TOTAL PRAISE

By

PROLIFIC, INTERNATIONAL BESTSELLING
AUTHOR

JOHN A. ANDREWS

AUTHOR OF

THE 5 PS FOR TEENS
QUOTES UNLIMITED
THE CHURCH ON FIRE
THE CHURCH … A HOSPITAL?
THE 5 STEPS TO CHANGING YOUR LIFE
SPREAD SOME LOVE - RELATIONSHIPS 101
DARE TO MAKE A DIFFERENCE-SUCCESS 101
&
TOTAL COMMITMENT-THE MINDSET OF CHAMPIONS

02/01/19

TOTAL PRAISE

Books That Will Enhance Your Life

A L I
Andrews Leadership International
                www.ALI Pictures.com
                www.JohnAAndrews.com

ISBN: **978-1721048861**
Cover Design: ALI
Front Cover Design: ALI
Edited by: ALI

TOTAL PRAISE

TOTAL PRAISE

¹Make a joyful noise unto the LORD, all ye lands.
²Serve the LORD with gladness: come before his presence with singing.
³Know ye that the LORD he is God: it is he that hath made us, and not we ourselves; we are his people, and the sheep of his pasture.
⁴Enter into his gates with thanksgiving, and into his courts with praise: be thankful unto him, and bless his name.
⁵For the LORD is good; his mercy is everlasting; and his truth endureth to all generations.

Psalm 100 King James Version (KJV)

TOTAL PRAISE

TABLE OF CONTENTS

TOTAL PRAISE

This book is dedicated to my mother, Elaine Louisa Andrews, who not only planted in me an appetite for God's word but lived a life of dedication and service to her church and community. Also to my sons Jonathan, Jefferri, and Jamison, who keep me filled with passion, persistence and purpose.

We are conditioned to praise God from whom all blessings flow only a limited basis. What a ladder climbing experience would occur in our lives if we gave him total praise? God wants your best and you should resolve early in life to never give anything but the best of which you are capable.

JOHN A. ANDREWS

CHAPTER **1**

IMAGINE IF YOU WERE SUFFERING from stage 4 cancer, and as your physician, I were to tell you that the cure for your almost fatal disease lies beneath the river bed. What if I prescribed that if you found, a little smooth rock, glittering as a diamond, placed it twice a day outside cancer infected area for one month, and you would be cured? What time would you wake up in the morning? What time would you arrive at the river bed? How diligent will be your search?

Camera! Lights! Action! As you look in the water, noticing several stones ruggedly, smoothly shaped, would you use a net or your bare hands, so you can feel the contour and identify of your cure easily?

In order to ensure your success and beat the odds, let's say you decided to use bare your hands instead of a net. You methodically fished. If sunset came and you didn't find it, now with blistered hands, would you return the following day to continue your search?

By now you have cleared almost all the stones from that river bed, but that special stone, your cure, was yet to be found. Not only are your hands aching and bloodied, but your back hurts severely. The sun sets again. You drag yourself home.

Now furious about the price you have paid thus far, you pick up the phone and call me complaining, "Where is that stone? I've looked all over; I'm sore. It's nowhere to be found."

And I respond, "Keep looking, the stone is there, plus you need to start medicating tomorrow."

Now you jump out of bed before the crack of dawn, so you can get to that river bed, fearing that a high tide of water will wash your medication away. You drag yourself to the river bed. You generalize…

Then right before sunset, with what little energy you have left, you clear more rocks from that river bed. Just when you were about to give up, you discovered the smooth stone - the cure for your disease.

Knowing that you have a whole month of treatment to go, you feel as though you've already been cured. You get on your ached knees in praise.

You call me back jubilantly. Forgetting the pain you've gone through, you shout out, "I've found it, I've found it! I love you, doctor. Thanks for saving my life." I respond, "What a thrill of success. You committed to the process and now you have success. YES! "

CHAPTER 2

UNFORTUNATELY, MOST SO-CALLED Christian leaders are more concerned about being politically correct than having the spirit of God embedded in their services. They seem to care more about losing their social standing and influence inside the church as well as the community. Some will even lie in order to mask their incompetence or insecurities. They create a smoke-screen.

They fasten themselves to the epiphany of denying the supernatural miraculous power of God. They lean on themselves. Their relationship with Him stagnates. Therefore, their praise is a dud. No matter how much they push it doesn't ascend beyond the roof of the sanctuary.

- Embroidered in their demise they forgot it was He who created the world and all things in it.

- They forgot it was He who parted the Red Sea, allowing access to the Children of Israel.

- They forgot He fed the Israelites with manna from Heaven, caused the water to gush forth from the rocks and quench their thirst.

- They forgot He showed His glory and led them through the wilderness with a cloud by day and fire by night.

- They forgot about His marvelous works in the past and in the present.

Most of those leaders are content; settling on buddying up and orchestrating cliques. They refrain from allowing the gifts of the Spirit to be manifested in their services. There is no sense of glory in it. They play church.

It must be noted that during Pentecost after those early disciples came together in one accord, they positioned themselves spiritually where the Holy Spirit could flow through them unhindered. They became electrified.

Old habits, old worn out customs of worship, inhibited methods of praise vanished. They became avail to have the Holy Spirit flow through and dwell within them. Thus, enhancing their lives so they can be radical, effective witness to their congregation and the world at large. They sing the praises "Not me but you Lord!" *Oh if our praise can touch those chords!*

God is in search of this brand. A brand of Christians who will praise Him to the utmost. A marque through whom He can fully manifest His power and His glory. He is looking for that free-flowing river instead of a pent-up dam. He is in search of Christians with that spiritual eyesight. A characteristic which can only be developed through a genuine relationship with Him. One created through prayer, fasting, and praise.

Sadly, if that relationship is not found soon He's prepared to rely on the rocks and stones to rise up and give Him praise.

CHAPTER 3

PRAISE MEANS TO COMMAND, to applaud, to magnify.

Lift Him up, the risen Savior,
High amid the waiting throng;
Lift Him up, 'tis He that speaketh,
Now He bids you flee from wrong.

Some Christians confuse praise with quietness. Thinking it's a form of reverence. Where one sits quietly and waits for God's spirit to flow through them.

On the other hand, some see it as dancing in the aisle and doing cartwheels in an extreme hallelujah breakdown.

Praise is a deep expression of worship. Where we raise our thoughts upwards and glorify God. It's an expression from the heart, humbling ourselves, centered on God with love, benevolence and thankfulness.

Jesus no doubt saw the hypocrisy of the Pharisees back then. Their worship was an outward show and not a feeling from the heart.

"This people draw nigh unto me with their mouth, and honoreth me with their lips, but their heart is far from me" (Matthew 15:8).

God wants genuine praise. Anything less wouldn't suffice because He delights in total love and devotion of His children.

Some Christians detest the sound of loud instruments. They can't relish the sound of the drums or even the tambourine. Set in their customs and comfort zone of quiet worship, if an instrument causes others to shake a little, those quiet worshippers are apt to leave the church and never return. They claim it's a worldly custom to be moved by music. They fail to realize praise is a lifestyle and not a loud sounding musical incident.

TOTAL PRAISE

Psalms 34:1 puts it this way, "I'll bless the Lord at all times: His praise shall continually be in my mouth."

THE BIBLE TELLS THE STORY regarding the unjust arrest of Paul and Silas. They had miraculously cast a spirit of divination out of a girl. As a result, the local Philippian authorities beat them and threw them into prison.

In addition to the trauma they suffered from severe administered beatings, they were fastened in stocks which clamped their arms and legs securely.

Circulation was therefore impeded, resulting in body cramps. The air inside that dungeon-like jail was rancid. As a result of improperly disposed waste. Their lungs by now became a wastebasket.

Yet, in spite of the throbbing pain and adverse condition therein. Paul and Silas not only prayed but sang praises to God.

It was a strange sound to those inmates. They probably were only accustomed to hearing groans as a result of beatings administered to their neighbors. On other occasions probably expletives mixed with threats.

Paul and Silas were no doubt accustomed to the attitude of lifting up their praise to God. A joyous presence emanated as they lift their voices to God. Songs like:

I serve a risen Savior

TOTAL PRAISE

He's in the world today.
I know that He is living,
Whatever men may say.
I see His hand of mercy;
I hear His voice of cheer;
And just the time I need Him
He's always near.

They provided God with a channel to intercede and operate in their circumstances. No wonder the foundations shook as an earthquake accompanied their praises. All the prison doors were opened and everyone's chains broke loose.

God dwells in the atmosphere of His praise. He is that vehicle of faith which takes us directly into His presence and power. It is said: Praise is the ticket which allows us to enter the sacredness to His glory.

We must understand: Worship is not a response after the Holy Spirit moves upon us but instead before it does so. According to Psalms 100:4, "Enter into his gates with thanksgiving, and into his courts with praise; be thankful unto him, and bless his name."

CHAPTER 4

AS HUMAN BEINGS, we are somewhat conditioned to holding onto. Even so, we have to step out of the box and overcome our negative, doubting, fearful and lethargic attitudes in order to embrace and dwell in the supernatural. It is only there, we ascend up to God and He comes down to meet us halfway. It is there, worthy praises materialize. Blessings are delivered, received and gratitude expressed.

TOTAL PRAISE

To praise God fully is to know Him. It's a miraculous experience to know Him. The knowledge that He wants nothing but our utmost. Half-a-praise won't do. He resides in the realm of abundance. Nothing which is done half hazardless will move him to action. He wants your all.

Your mind affects the attitudes you develop whether in the darkroom or under the mid-day sun. The thought pattern you've developed over the years can hinder you from the miraculous. If you believe in miracles, miracles will supernaturally emerge in your habitat. You'll shout constantly, "I'm blessed…"

First, you must bring every thought and place it in subjection to the will of Christ. It is there your "aha" moment encircles. Lifting you to higher heights.

One who is in constant, utmost praise to God is apt to develop supernatural eyesight. That ability to see, perceive and understand things beyond the natural realm. They are able to see in the unlimited, immeasurable richness of God's power and His glory. They can pray into one's affairs and it's granted… So that when they would walk by, their shadow would fall on them and heal them or healed by touching their used handkerchief. The miraculous occurs. Yet, we must realize: It's not us who are doing the works of God; it is Christ, who is living in us. Therefore, having a revelation of Christ, we see Him as He is and what seems impossible becomes possible.

TOTAL PRAISE

Many churches today remain in a stagnant, lethargic state because their praise is superficial, counterfeited and unbalanced. Their faith lacks patina. Many in need of miracles doubt He can deliver. Even so, knowingly, He's able to do what He says he can do. Knowingly, He can provide all of your needs: monetarily, wellness, a clean heart or otherwise. Whatever circumstance you face, He can deliver and bless you if you exhibit an attitude of total praise and confidence in Him.

CHAPTER 5

IN ORDER TO RECEIVE MIRACLES, we must put our faith into action. It is said: "Faith without works is dead." If we know our position of kingdom dominance we would walk in it. We're made in God's image. With that said, we ought to take up our position of power and authority over any satanic power. Principalities will not be able to shackle us. Since praise is known to manifest God's presence, we must in confidence realize that praise repels satanic powers.

TOTAL PRAISE

We were made for miracles and miracles were made for us. Just like the Children of Israel, Daniel, Shadrach, Meshach, and Abednego, The Shunammite Woman, Abraham and Sarah, Elisha, and the benefactors of Jesus' constellation of miracles. How their praise must have ascended up mixed with overwhelming joy and thanksgiving.

God created us through His supernatural manifestation and power. He still operates through that domain. He spoke and it was done. He commanded and it stood fast.

You must understand that you were made for miracles and God is ever present, willing and able to manifest His power in your circumstances. However, it must be understood that your praise is the magical component which moves Him.

As we praise totally, we are able to break down every hindrance which stands in our way and summons the flow of God's power and glory. When we praise wholly we encounter a breakthrough with our name on it. Our next move is to take action in order to claim it.

You may have to break through your own living environment, which may include your thoughts, your imaginations, your emotions, your negative attitudes, your preconceived ideas and your circumstances. What you see, hear and speak even your ability to praise him to the utmost formulates that composite.

TOTAL PRAISE

You must understand that you fight against principalities and powers which serves as a dam; preventing your flow from taking its course.

Most of us go through life depending on our own abilities to move those mountains which exist or will cunningly present themselves from time to time. We become bound by our natural abilities which hinder us from accessing God's supernatural power.

Our praise is weak. If it doesn't move us, would it be that powerful to move God? Highly impossible... One writer puts it this way: *As long as you remain bound by the natural, it is impossible to walk in the supernatural and take hold of the miracles you need. Once you have broken through your natural limitations, however, you will be able to live in an atmosphere whereby you can experience miracles in every area of your life.*

John 4:24 states: "God is Spirit, and those who worship Him must worship in spirit and truth."

CHAPTER 6

PRIOR TO 911 which hit New York City with severity. I was getting acclimated to Hollywood after my acting tenure in NYC tenure. Still sinking my teeth in Tinsel Town, a Los Angeles talent agent signed me commercially. In that infancy stage, several national TV campaigns were hurried into my catalog. This brought smiles to my agent, my family, my friends and me. So much that like flies caught in a trap, my headshots lit up the walls of that boutique Hollywood Commercial Agency.

Then the world trade financial towers were hit by terrorists. Weeks following that NYC crisis, with smoke still rising from those ruins, the advertising milieu declined. That successful TV campaign running streak dried up. After moonlighting with a modeling agent I went solo.

I opened a modeling agency in the heart of Hollywood. In less than a year I grew it to a thirty-five talent roster. My wall looked great. Jobs were coming in. Yet, attitudinally, models struggled. They became lethargic preferring the big auditions and premiere bookings. However, those were customarily far and in between. As a result, the agency suffered and looking myself in the mirror, I realized it was time to move on to greener pastures.

One night, while navigating the TV channels, a movie began rolling out its opening credits. It caught my attention. So I fetched a Jamaican Soda and reclined in the chair to watch this flick. Not only was I intrigued. I critiqued, saw not only the holes inside the script and in the directing as well.

"How did this movie get made?" I questioned. The end credits rolled and I powered off the small screen. My eyelids became heavy and sleep beckoned. However, my mind stayed awake roaming creatively. If only... If only...

TOTAL PRAISE

Jumping out of bed the next morning, I became affixed to the yellow pages and the landline phone. That rut lasted for almost three weeks without success.

On a subsequent call, a woman on the other end of the line fessed up. They totally owned the rights to my pending pet project. After telling her about my interest in acquiring those rights. I sensed a decline in her voice.

"We are not interested in giving up those rights to a third party."

"Miss_____, I've researched the film and fell we could collaborate on making it better."

"Sorry, we are not interested parting with those rights." She reminded me, just in case my ears were waxed laden. The boss woman had to go. I immediately went to work as a result of that rejection. First, I call to my screenwriter friend who had his latest script optioned by a major film studio. He wanted to assist totally. Even so, he was boxed in with a conflict of interest: He was signed to a manager and held a ghostwriting clause was not in my favor. In any event, he emailed me some screenwriting templates and instructed:

"Go for it!"

I did!

In twenty-nine days my first screenplay was etched. After jumping up like a kid inside a candy store. I rushed it off to my ex-acting coach. His resume included directing some Hollywood mega-stars.

TOTAL PRAISE

About a month later, he emailed me. "Nice he read it!" I entertained until the body of the email mirrored his bluntness and satire. "John, this is the worse screenplay I've ever read. You are such a novice at it. This is entirely not for you."

Subsequently, seven sleepless days and nights haunted me. Finally, I dusted myself off, powered up my computer and continued writing.

A year later, I sent a follow-up screenplay to my now critic. Days later, my phone rang. It was him!

"Mate!" he said in his Australian dialect.

"How are you?"

I responded.

"I've reviewed your work and it looks darn good."

"Really?"

I asked.

"It has a story to it. Not too many actions flick contain a great story. Most of them are just shoot them up ... Bang! Bang!"

"Thanks much,"

I responded. While on the inside my spirits echoed: "Praise God! Praise God! Praise be to God!"

It was there I knew for certain... Nobody was going to stop me from writing.

So I embarked upon writing up a massive body of work.

CHAPTER 7

IN 2007, MY FIRST BOOK was etched. The 5 Steps to Changing Your Life. In one week the first draft was finished. A writer who was not able to master the keyboard and crawled as a one-handed-one finger typist had accomplished the miraculous. The following year momentum mixed with supernatural miracles kicked in and I give birth to eight books in less than ten calendar months.

TOTAL PRAISE

The following year my first novel, Rude Bauy was released and accompanied me on the road – cross country. In less than two months on that circuit, the title soared to become a national bestseller.

Because of Rude Buay, its sequels and other titles, I've traveled to book signing events in almost every US state, including the territory of Puerto Rico.

In 2016, my trips included film festivals in Hong Kong and Cannes, France for coming to film previews. During August of that same year, the Jamaican Government invited me in for a 7-Day Jamaican tour in order to scout filming locations.

In early 2017, the Jamaican Stock Exchange invited me in as their wrap-up speaker at their annual investor's conference. There I've shared the stage with regional heads of governments as well as investors.

At the tail-end of that trip, we completed round two of our location scouting.

Returning from Jamaica I delved in and revaluated my blessings. "Praise be to God," I exclaimed upon boarding that American Airlines flight back to the US. Consequently, books 37 & 38 The Church ... A Hospital? and The Church On Fire entered my catalog. As a result, I stepped into the director's seat and moved the duo to Off-Broadway.

"My Utmost for His Highest,"

I say…for his miraculous supernatural intervention in my affairs.

TOTAL PRAISE

Miracles, which for me I could never see myself as life's occurrences.

It is said:

"God opens the spiritual of those who are hungry for Him and yielded to Him."

CHAPTER 8

AS A STRUGGLING ACTOR in Hollywood. I drove limousines part time and would occasionally run errands for a branded film producer.

I rented an apartment way up in the Malibu Hills. It was not only affordable but presented me with inordinate creative optics. I cherished that panoramic view of the Pacific Ocean.

TOTAL PRAISE

Almost three miles from the Pacific Coast Highway, that scenery was in a league by itself. The only drawback was rolling rocks. Occasionally, a few of them dislodged and created temporary roadblocks.

My silver 626 Mazda acclimated to those winding roads along the hillside. Additionally, my creativity had stepped up multiple levels. I read. I wrote. I meditated. I praised.

One Sunday, I traveled to the San Fernando Valley. On the way back my car decided it didn't want to go any further. A mechanic looked at it and determined repairing it would be futile. It had given up the ghost.

Stranded almost thirty miles from home plus those Hills to climb without transportation was not an easy chore. I praised God in the fact that it wasn't me who was inoperable.

A Good Samaritan showed up and on that hot California day. He gladly transported me back to the Hills of Malibu.

The following day, the producer's girlfriend called me. They had errands to run. I told her I was car-less. She empathized. She had previously lived not too far from where I resided.

The next morning, the producer called me and recommended I visit a familiar car dealership and locate a good used car. Hours later, a friend showed up and transported me to the car mart. I picked out an automobile within his proposed $10,000.00 budget. Moments later he wired a check to the dealership for the payment. The title car was issued. My friend hi-fived me. Boarded her car and drove away.

After the car was washed and vacuumed and simonized, I drove away from the dealership in high God Almighty Praise.

ABOUT A YEAR LATER, my magical producer friend was in the process of releasing an independent film. There was no big-name talent in the cast. He invited me to his Hollywood office. He was busy but he went out his way to accommodate my visit. His assistant walked me right in to see him. He was on the phone. I took a seat.

He briskly wrapped up the call and began to pow-wow. He explained the film's scenario. After which he climaxed:

"Regarding its potential. I'm keeping my fingers crossed."

Weeks later, I attended his film's premiere. It was well attended. The previous night it premiered in New York City and attracted rave reviews. There was now a buzz in the air and it was ear tingling.

On that opening weekend, it grossed $35M in Box Office sales. Months later it drew worldwide sales over $100,000.00 USD.

Every installment since, it has grossed similar profits worldwide.

TOTAL PRAISE

He has since, not only invested heavily in real estate, stocks and other movies but relocated from Sherman Oaks to an elite Hollywood neighborhood.

CHAPTER 9

ONE MORNING I ATTENDED a church service in Hollywood, California. It was church as usual except there was some undercurrent amongst the leadership. I could tell from their body language there was an indication of great concern.

After the praise team sang their hearts out and the congregation gave a standing ovation. The senior pastor took to the stage. He summoned the other pastors in attendance as they formed a huddle. He asked for his wife to join them and she did.

Tongue tied, he announced she had been diagnosed with breast cancer. You could hear a pin drop in that theatre style sanctuary.

Next, he asked those huddled on stage to each pray on her behalf. The rest of the congregation to pray silently. He preached that day. It was a different kind of sermon than we've been accustomed to. His message was one of praise for all that God had done for him and his family.

Time elapsed and during the weeks which followed he updated the church on her condition. He mentioned how he was tired of wheatgrass because that was always on the breakfast menu. He also said his wife had been in prayer continuously. Additionally, she had been living, breathing these positive affirmations and others which she etched on multiple index cards:

- No weapon formed against me shall prosper.

- "I can do all things through Christ which strengtheneth me." (Phil. 4:13 KJV)

- "The steps of a good *woman* are ordered by the Lord." (Ps. 37:23 KJV)

- I refuse to renounce my self-image, no matter what happens to me.

TOTAL PRAISE

- The battle is not mine; it belongs to the Lord.

- What God has for me no devil in hell can take.

- I was born to fight this.

- The time has come for my change.

- God is taking me where no woman has gone before.

- I must beat cancer.

- I can have what God says I can have.

- I will arise! I will finish.

- When it's all said and done, I'll come out of it.

- I'm the head and not the tail.

- You may whip some but not me. I'm going to force you to give up.

- I have what it takes to fight cancer.

- I'm a giant killer.

- I'm chosen. I can take less and do more with it.

- God wants me to be so blessed that I live in the land of much.

- God is opening doors for me that no one can shut.

Months passed. Not only did she avoid the process of chemotherapy but she was cured of that life-threatening disease. It has been over seventeen years ago and she is still in the best of health and witnessing for the Lord.

CHAPTER 10

THE CHILDREN OF ISRAEL had been suppressed into slavery by Pharaoh and the Egyptians. For years they would not let God's people go. So He rained ten plagues upon the Egyptians. Then He entrusted Moses with the task of leading the Israelites to the Promised Land.

As they journeyed, through the wilderness, barred by the Red Sea, Pharaoh pursued them along with his armies with six hundred choice chariots, with captains over every one of them. He wanted them to "walk it back." But when Pharaoh drew near, they lifted their eyes, they beheld the wilderness and the Red Sea. They feared and cried out to Moses: "Let us alone so we may serve the Egyptians." He told them: "Don't be afraid. Stand still, and see the salvation of the Lord, which He will accomplish for you today. For the Egyptians whom you see today, you shall see them no more forever. The Lord will fight for you, and you shall hold your peace." (Exodus 14: 13-14).

Moses, no doubt still complained to God, Who responded. "Why do you cry to me? Tell the children of Israel to go forward. But lift up your rod, and stretch out your hand over the sea and divide it. And the children of Israel shall go through it onto dry land." (Exodus 14:15-16).

Moses did!

As a result, God parted the Red Sea. Pharaoh and his armies pursued. They were swallowed up as the sea recalibrated after the children of Israel passed through.

DURING THE REIGN of King Nebuchadnezzar, he erected a golden image and commanded the three Hebrew boys: Shadrach, Meshach, and Abednego to bow down and worship it. They refused.

The king commanded his underlings to make the furnace exceeding hot. So much the fire slew those who threw in the trio inside the fiery furnace.

TOTAL PRAISE

As the fire continued burning, hotter and hotter, another individual appeared standing in those flames and among the three Hebrew Boys. "Did we not cast three men bound into the midst of the fire? He asked his counselors. They answered: "Yes." He responded: Lo, I see four men loose, walking in the midst of the fire, and they have no hurt; and the form of the fourth is like the Son of God."

As Nebuchadnezzar soaked up the optics he came near to the mouth of that fiery furnace and said: "Shadrach, Meshach, and Abednego, ye servants of the most high God, come forth and come hither. Then Shadrach, Meshach and Abednego came forth in the midst of the fire." Not a hair on their bodies was singed, neither were their coats changed, not even the smell of fire emanated from them.

DANIEL, A PROPHET OF GOD was presented with a decree that the people should pray only to the Persian king for thirty days. On the other hand, Daniel, a law-abiding man, continued praying to God as he had always done before. The evil men who instigated the decree did so in the first place to entrap Daniel. They reported it to Darius.

Now forced to put Daniel in the lion's den. King Darius said: "May your God whom you serve continually, rescue you." (Daniel 6:16).

TOTAL PRAISE

God did indeed rescue Daniel, sending his angels to shut up the mouth of the lions so they couldn't harm him.

CHAPTER 11

IN THE DAYS OF ELISHA, a rich woman lived in a town called Shunem. Whenever Elisha came to visit Shunem, she invited him to eat with them. There he also found a place to rest his weary feet. The woman was overly kind to Elisha because she knew he was a holy man of God. So much that she and her husband made a bedroom for him on their roof so he can have a place to stay whenever he was in town.

On this particular visit. He went up to his room to rest awhile. In the interim, he told his servant Gehazi to go get the Shunammite woman. He did. There she was. Elisha feeling a strong desire to bless hcr. He said to her:

"You have gone to a lot of trouble for us. Now, what can we do for you? Can we speak to the king for you? Or can we speak to the commander for you?"

"I live among my own people. I have everything I need here."

She responded, then turned and left.

When she was gone, Elisha asked Gehazi:

"What can we do for her?"

Thinking deeply, Gehazi responded:

"Well, she doesn't have a son. And her husband is old."

Elisha commanded:

"Bring her again."

He did. She stood there in the doorway.

"You will hold a son in your arms. It would be about this time next year." Elisha said.

"No, my master! You are a man of God. So don't lie to me!"

She objected. No doubt she has been hurt before by those who led her on.

TOTAL PRAISE

Sure enough. She became pregnant. One year later, she was holding her new baby boy in her hand. Just like Elisha had said.

As the boy grew. His father took him to the fields. No doubt to learn the art of farming. He said to his dad: "My head hurts! It really hurts!"

His dad told a servant who eavesdropped in desperation to carry him to his mother. He did!

The boy sat on his lap until evening. Unfortunately, he died. She hurried up to the room on the roof. Lay him down on Elisha's bed. Shut the door and went out. How she must have prayed in earnestness. Nothing changed.

She sent a message to her husband in the field via a servant.

"Please send me one of the servants and a donkey. Then I can go quickly to the man of God and return."

Her husband questioned why she wanted to go to Elisha, she didn't answer. Stating there was nothing to worry about. How he must have praised in advance while she rode to Mount Carmel to find Elisha.

Elisha saw him from a distance and sent a servant to see if she was okay. She let the servant know she was alright. However, when she got to Elisha, she fell to his feet.

Elisha must have seen evidence of dismay in the depths of her soul.

"Master, did I ask you for a son? Didn't I tell you, Don't get my hopes up?"

She said.

Elisha said to his servant Gehazi,

"Tuck your coat into your belt. Take my wooden staff and run to Shunem. Don't say hello to anyone you see. If anyone says hello to you, don't answer. Lay my staff on the boy's face.

The boy's mother said,

"I won't leave you. And that's just as sure as the Lord and you are alive."

That became resonant with Elisha. So he got up and followed her. Gehazi led the way. He laid Elisha's wooden staff on the boy's face. Not only was there no sound coming from the boy but he didn't move at all.

Gehazi rushed back to Elisha and updated him on the boy's status.

Elisha arrived at the woman's house. The boy was still dead and lying on Elisha's bed. Elisha went into the room. Shut the door. Alone with the boy, he prayed to God. Then he spread out over the boy. Suddenly, the boy's body began to get warm. Frantically, Elisha walked back and forth across the floor. Then he repeated the former process.

The boy sneezed seven times and suddenly opened his eyes.

Elisha called for the boy's mother. Upon her arrival, Elisha said:

"Take your son."

TOTAL PRAISE

She entered fell on her knees at Elisha's feet in total praise. Her heart overflowing with gratitude and praise.

CHAPTER 12

JESUS LEFT HIS GLORY ABOVE and came to earth. His ultimate objective to seek and save the lost. In so doing, He never forgot whose mission He was on. Thus, multitudes were reminded: It was His Father who sent Him.

During His expedition. He not only replaced a severed ear. Set the captive free. Brought healing to the sick.

Comforted the distressed. Turned water into wine. Drove out evil spirits. Raised the dead. Calmed the angry sea. Gave sight to the blind. Fed the multitude. Cleansed the lepers. Walked on water. These incidents were documented by multiple eye-witnesses.

In His constellation of miracles. Thirty-Seven of which were recorded in the four gospels. His announcement was mandated:

"If you can believe, all things are possible to him who believes." Mark 9:23.

His thirty-seven miracles are listed in chronological order:

MIRACLES.	WHERE WROUGHT.	WHERE RECORDED.
Water made wine	Cana	Joh 2:1-11.
Traders cast out of the temple	Jerusalem	Joh 2:13-17.
Nobleman's son healed	Cana	Joh 4:46-54.
First miraculous draught of fishes	Sea of Galilee	Lu 5:1-11.
Leper healed	Capernaum	Mt 8:2-4; Mark 1:40-45; Lu 5:12-15.
Centurion's servant healed	Capernaum	Mt 8:5-13; Lu 7:1-10.
Widow's son raised to life	Nain	Lu 7:11-17.
Demoniac healed	Capernaum	Mr 1:21-28; Lu 4:31-37.

Peter's mother-in-law healed	Capernaum	Mt 8:14, 15; Mr 1:29-31; Lu 4:38, 39.
Paralytic healed	Capernaum	Mt 9:2-8; Mr 2:1-12; Lu 5:17-26.
Impotent man healed	Jerusalem	Joh 5:1-16.
Man with withered hand healed	Galilee	Mt 12:10-14; Mr 3:1-6; Lu 6:6-11.
Blind and dumb demoniac healed	Galilee	Mt 12:22-24; Lu 11:14.
Tempest stilled	Sea of Galilee	Mt 8:23-27; Mr 4:35-41; Lu 8:22-25.
Demoniacs dispossessed	Gadara	Mt 8:28-34; Mr 5:1-20.
Jairus' daughter raised to life	Capernaum	Mt 9:18-26; Mr 5:22-24; Lu 8:41-56.
Issue of blood healed	Near Capernaum	Mt 9:18-26; Mr 5:22-24; Lu 8:41-56.
Two blind men restored to sight	Capernaum	Mt 9:27-31.
Dumb demoniac healed	Capernaum	Mt 9:32-34.
Five thousand miraculously fed	Decapolis	Mt 14:13-21; Mr 6:31-44; Lu 9:10-17; Joh 6:5-14.
Jesus walks on the sea	Sea of Galilee	Mt 14:22-33; Mr 6:45-52; Joh 6:15-21.
Syrophœnician's daughter healed	Coasts of Tyre and Sidon	Mt 15:21-28; Mr 7:24-30.

Deaf and dumb man healed	Decapolis	Mr 7:31-37.
Four thousand fed	Decapolis	Mt 15:32-39; Mr 8:1-9.
Blind man restored to sight	Bethsaida	Mr 8:22-26.
Demoniac and lunatic boy healed	Near Cæsarea Philippi	Mt 17:14-21; Mr 9:14-29; Lu 9:37-43.
Miraculous provision of tribute	Capernaum	Mt 17:24-27.
The eyes of one born blind opened	Jerusalem	Joh 9:1-41.
Woman, of eighteen years' infirmity, cured	[Perea.]	Lu 13:10-17.
Dropsical man healed	[Perea.]	Lu 14:1-6.
Ten lepers cleansed	Borders of Samaria	Lu 17:11-19.
Lazarus raised to life	Bethany	Joh 11:1-46.
Two blind beggars restored to sight	Jericho	Mt 20:29-34; Mr 10:46-52; Lu 18:35-43.
Barren fig tree blighted	Bethany	Mt 21:12, 13, 18, 19; Mr 11:12-24.

Buyers and sellers again cast out	Jerusalem	Lu 19:45, 46.
Malchus' ear healed	Gethsemane	Mt 26:51-54; Mr 14:47-49; Lu 22:50, 51; Joh 18:10,11.
Second draught of fishes	Sea of Galilee	Joh 21:1-14.

It must be noted, none of those eclectic 37 documented miracles were performed for enjoyment or for a spectacle. Each was carried out or accompanied by a special message.

Most of all each met a special, specific need. *Each also identified his authority as the Son of God.*

We find that there were times when he refused from going into His miraculous zone, not because of His inability to produce results but because they did not conform to the precedent.

Accordingly, when Herod saw Jesus, he was very glad, for he long desired to see Him. You see, he had heard about Jesus and was hoping to witness a sign performed by Him. So he questioned Jesus at length, but Jesus answered him not. (Luke 23:8-9). Just before His crucifixion, it was recorded: He replaced a severed ear. Subsequently, He hung dying on the cross. He could have come down from that cross, heal the wounds in His hands and feet, destroy those Roman soldiers and set Himself free. Yet, He did not!

CHAPTER 13

WE FIND THAT SOME of Jesus' most astonishing miracles included: restoring sight to the blind, casting out demons, healing the sick, bringing the dead back to life, feeding the multitudes, turning water into wine and walking on water. Because of His supernatural expressions of love, many were drawn to Him. He revealed His divinity, opened their hearts to salvation and most notably caused God to be glorified.

TOTAL PRAISE

It is a requisite: In everything we do, let God be glorified. The praises must go up in order for the blessings to come down.

Inside most of our churches today, many get uncomfortable whenever, a member who has been shipwrecked, tossed and turned to cajole their disappointments in life, decides to praise God to their utmost. They readily reject the member, preferring him or her resort to a quiet, menial form of praise. Even though within that member reflecting how God has done the supernatural in their lives and within the spirit cries out: *Let God be glorified!*

"Make a joyful noise unto the Lord." Give Him the glory and see, because of your gratitude the miraculous occurrences which unfold. Showers of blessings will quench your thirsty soul. You will be lifted to higher heights.

IT WAS ON A SABBATH DAY. Jesus followed a crowd in tow and arrived in Capernaum. There He entered into the temple and proceeded to expound with authority. The congregation was astonished at His doctrine. Mainly because He taught them as one who had authority. Much different from the scribes who possessed a form of godliness but denied the power thereof. To say the least, they were moved. So much that they saw in Him an entity who can do anything.

TOTAL PRAISE

Inside the temple lay a man with an unclean spirit. From inside the man, a voice cried out: "Let us alone. What have we to do with thee, thou Jesus of Nazareth? Art thou come to destroy us?"

After those two questions, he continued: "I know thee who thou art The Holy One of God."

Jesus immediately rebuked the devil saying: "Hold thy peace and come out of him."

The unclean spirit tore the man as it escaped.

Those gathered cried with a loud voice as this miracle unfolded: "He came out of him."

In the interim, they questioned amongst themselves and retorted: "What thing is this? For with authority commandeth He even the unclean spirits, and they obey Him."

The man, however, was not hurt during the unclean spirit's removal process. Instead one can only imagine how he praised and glorified extensively.

CHAPTER 14

PRECEDING ANOTHER MIRACULOUS encounter, Jesus, while in the company of Jairus a crowd thronged him. He stopped to help a woman amongst them who had an issue of blood for twelve years. When the woman had heard of Jesus, she came in behind and touched His garment.

Jairus, knowing his daughter was sick probably wished Jesus would hurry up and proceed to his house.

TOTAL PRAISE

The woman said: "If I may touch but his clothes, I shall be whole.

And straightway the fountain of her blood was dried up, and she felt in her body that she was healed of that plague.

And Jesus, immediately knowing in himself that virtue had gone out of him, turned him about in the press, and said, Who touched my clothes?"

His disciples, also present responded: "Thou seest the multitude thronging thee, and sayest thou, Who touched me?

32 And he looked round about to see her that had done this thing.

33 But the woman fearing and trembling, knowing what was done in her, came and fell down before him, and told him all the truth.

34 And he said unto her, Daughter, thy faith hath made thee whole; go in peace and be whole of thy plague.

During this delay, several men from Jairus' house emerged and reported to Jesus that Jairus' daughter is dead.

When they arrived at the house, Jesus tells them not to cry because she is not dead. How they laughed at Jesus. One could only imagine the looks on their faces. He said the same thing as was said about Lazarus: "She is only asleep.

This miracle was a testament to his father's power, manifested to those allowed to witness this: Jairus' family, and His disciples. As her spirit returned Jesus instructed she be given something to eat. Showing concern for details; one could only eat if he or she is alive.

On the other hand, the delay in following Jairus resulted in more glory to God in that Jesus instead of just healing Jairus' daughter he raised her from the dead and cured the woman with the issue of blood.

CHAPTER 15

AFTER JESUS RAISED JAIRUS' DAUGHTER back to life. His fame went through the land. As He sojourned, two blind men followed Him crying:

"Thou Son of David have mercy on me."

According to the account in Matthew 9:28-34,

28And when he was come into the house, the blind men came to him: and Jesus saith unto them, Believe ye that I am able to do this? They said unto him, Yea, Lord.

29Then touched he their eyes, saying, According to your faith be it unto you.

30And their eyes were opened; and Jesus straitly charged them, saying, See *that* no man know *it*.

31But they, when they were departed, spread abroad his fame in all that country.

32As they went out, behold, they brought to him a dumb man possessed with a devil.

33And when the devil was cast out, the dumb spake: and the multitudes marveled, saying, It was never so seen in Israel.

34But the Pharisees said, He casteth out devils through the prince of the devils.

It was recorded, later, Jesus went about all the cities and villages, teaching, preaching the gospel of the kingdom and healing every sickness and disease among the people. Beholding the multitudes who had come to see Him. He was moved with compassion upon them because they fainted and were scattered abroad as sheep having no shepherd. Exhorting His disciples He said:

"The harvest truly is plenteous but the laborers are few: Pray ye therefore, the Lord of the harvest, that He will send forth laborers into His harvest."

In these end times, it's obvious the harvest is ripened. Yet, we are esteemed laborers with Him? Do we maintain a genuine relationship with Him? Are our praises so low thereby causing our blessings to remain on high?

CHAPTER 16

DAVID, IN THE OLD TESTAMENT, was classified as a man after God's own heart. Yet, he was caught in a downward spiral of sin. As we recount the story:

It was late one afternoon when David arose from his couch and went walking on the roof of the king's house. He saw a woman bathing; she was very beautiful. David could not resist her beauty and sent and inquired about her. And one said, "Is not this Bathsheba, the daughter of Eliam, the wife of Uriah the Hittite? So David sent messengers and took her and she came to him, and he took her…Then she returned to her house. And the woman conceived, and she sent and told David, "I am pregnant."

David looking for a twist in the story and trying to cover up his sin and sought Uriah her husband from battle so Uriah could lie with her and think it was his baby. Uriah, on the other hand, was too noble to go into his wife while his comrades were engaged in battle. So David arranged to have him killed so he David could quickly marry Bathsheba and cover up the act of adultery.

It was said: "The thing that David did displeased the Lord" (2 Samuel 11:27). So God sent the prophet Nathan to David with a parable which entices David to pronounce his own condemnation. Nathan, cleverly says: "You are the man!" and further asks, "Why have you despised the word of the Lord?" David breaks out into confession, "I have sinned against the Lord." Nathan replied astonishingly, "The Lord has put away your sin; you shall not die. Nevertheless, because by this deed you have utterly scorned the Lord, the child who is born to you shall die" (2 Samuel 12:7-15).

In this sequence of events: Bathsheba is raped. Uriah is dead. The Baby will die. Yet Nathan told David,

"The Lord has put away your sin." Let's recount just in case you missed it. David committed adultery. He ordered the execution of Uriah. He also lied. Yet, the God stepped in and forgave him of those sins. David, forgiven for those sins is now made whole in the sight of God. Is this supernatural or is it supernatural? We are told in Psalms 51, David cried out to God:

Firstly, David turns to his only hope. "Have mercy upon me, O God, according to your steadfast love; according to your abundant mercy blot out my transgressions." We find here in Verse 1, mercy was solicited three times: *Have mercy, according to your steadfast love* and *according to your abundant mercy.*

Secondly, David prays for cleansing. Verse 2: "Wash me thoroughly from my iniquity, and cleanse me from my sin." Verse 7: Purge me with hyssop, and I shall be clean; wash me, and I shall be whiter than snow." Whiter than snow is a far cry by any stretch of one's imagination.

Thirdly, David confesses the seriousness of his sin possibly by counting all five fingers on his left hand while kneeling before God.

1. Verse 3: "For I know my transgressions, and my sin is ever before me."

2. Verse 4: "Against you, you only, have I sinned and done this evil in your sight."
3. Verse 4: …so that you may be justified in your words and blameless in your judgment."
4. Verse 5: "Behold I was brought forth in iniquity, and in sin did my mother conceive me."
5. Verse 6: 'Behold, you delight in truth in the inward being, and you teach me wisdom in the secret heart."

David, you see had been a man after God's own heart but sin got the upper hand. Psalms 51 continues, with him pleading for renewal.

"A broken spirit and a contrite heart God will not despise."

CHAPTER **17**

A CERTAIN MAN RAISED A SON in Jesus' day who was demon possessed. The demon caused him to convulse, foam at the mouth and grind his teeth. The father brought him in search of Jesus to be healed. Jesus was missing in action and he ran into His disciples. Not only was the man's faith weak but also that of the disciples. The disciples who had spent a tenure with Jesus sat with Him and learned from Him.

Yet, they were unable to cast out the demon. Subsequently, the spent their time arguing with the evangelicals of their time, in order to mask their ineptness.

When Jesus arrived on the scene, He asked them what they were arguing about. (Mark 9:16). The man who had brought his son to be healed explained their inability to heal the kid.

Rebuking those gathered Jesus said:

"O faithless generation, how long shall I be with you? How long shall I bear with you? Bring him to me."(Mark 9:19).

It was evident the reason for the child's uncooperativeness to healing was mainly because of their unbelief.

Jesus asked the father: "How long has this been happening?"

"From childhood. And often he had thrown him into fire and water to destroy him. But if you can do anything have compassion on us and help us." (Mark 9:21-22).

The man in sincerity asked earnestly and Jesus delivered abundantly. His praises went up and the blessings came down.

JESUS, WHILE TRAVELING along the border of Samaria and Galilee, came into this village and met a group of people suffering from leprosy. They stood at a distance and called out in a loud voice, "Jesus,

Master, have pity on us!" Jesus had compassion on them and said: "Go, show yourselves to the priests," They journeyed and were cleansed. It is a known fact if one were to touch a leper, he or she stands the risk of contracting leprosy. No wonder they cried out: *have pity on us*! It is evident no one came near or dared to associate themselves with that disease spreading victims.

One of them, a Samaritan, when he realized he was cleansed of this incurable variety of skin diseases, he returned, threw himself at Jesus' feet and thanked him. Jesus asked, Were not all ten cleansed? Where are the other nine? Has no one returned to give praise except this foreigner?"(Luke 17:17-18 NIV). The cleansed leper, no doubt, lingered at Jesus' feet; in penitence realizing his allies who he must have hung out with for years, refused to show gratitude to the one who had cured them, by at least saying *Thanks*. However, Jesus said to him,

"Rise up and go; your faith has made you well." (Luke 17:19 NIV).

How the once a "leper" and now cleansed must have leaped for joy, offering praises up to God.

CHAPTER 18

ONE DAY, JESUS and his disciples, while departing from Bethany, he saw a fig tree in the distance. The tree (as the story was told in the Gospels of Matthew and Mark) had leaves on it, plus Jesus was hungry. So he went to see if the tree had any fruit on it. When he got there, he found nothing but leaves on it. Naturally, it was not the season for figs. Jesus then said to the tree,

"May no one ever eat from you again,"

His disciples, present, heard it. This was yet another in Jesus' repertoire of 40 miracles.

In the morning as they continued their journey, they saw the fig tree withered from its roots. Peter, not forgetting yesterday's miraculous encounter, said to Jesus, "Rabbi, look! The tree you cursed has withered!"

"Have faith in God,"

Jesus answered.

"Truly I tell you, if anyone says to this mountain, 'Go, throw yourself into the sea,' and does not doubt in your heart but believe what they say will happen, it will be done to them.

Therefore I tell you, whatever you ask for in prayer, believe that you have received it, and it will be yours. And when you stand praying, if you hold anything against anyone, forgive them, so that your Father in heaven may forgive you your sins." (Mark 11:12-14; 20-25 NIV).

Forgiveness is a very prominent theme in the Bible. If you include words like *forgive* and *forgiven* and similar derivatives it occurs 116 times. In the Lord's Prayer, the noun *forgive* is found twice along with the noun **kingdom**.

Forgiveness, no doubt is a prerequisite for entering into God's kingdom. If we aren't willing to forgive others, why do we think our heavenly Father would forgive us when we sin. Whenever we choose not to forgive one another, it's like refusing to free ourselves from that vice which the one who has wronged us is also tightly squeezed into.

It might be alarming to know that many adults go to their graves holding onto un-forgiveness from since they were of childhood years. They refuse to live a life free from the guilt of un-forgiveness. Therefore, content with carrying the onus of not forgiving they die in resentfulness and misery.

The Lord's Prayer

Our Father who art in heaven, hallowed be thy name. Thy kingdom come. Thy will be done on earth as it is in heaven. Give us this day our daily bread, and forgive us our trespasses, as we forgive those who trespass against us, and lead us not into temptation, but deliver us from evil.

For thine is the kingdom, and the power, and the glory, forever and ever.

Amen.

CHAPTER 19

DURING JESUS' TENURE HERE on earth, the scribes and Pharisees among others were notorious for tempting and testing his alignment with God. It seems as if his cleansing power and actions were always on trial. They pressured him on everything: including what was lawful to do on the Sabbath day, who had access to Heaven, who he should dine with, the powers he possessed, the Law of Moses, the authenticity of his miracles, whose Son was he and much more.

One day, they brought unto him a woman taken in adultery, and sat her down in his midst. "They said unto him, Master, this woman was taken in adultery, in the very act. Now the law of Moses counseled that such should be stoned: but what sayest thou?" (John 8:3-4).

It was clear to Jesus they were once again tempting him as they had done on numerous occasions. It was apparent some of them if not all of them were involved in an adulterous act with the woman. Now, they were even referring to her as "such."

Jesus, the master at human relations didn't at this point clear his throat but stooped down, and with his finger wrote on the ground, pretending he hadn't heard them. His actions must have ticked them off. Plus, it seemed at first his message wasn't vividly clear to them. So they pressed him with the rhetorical question. *Now the law of Moses counseled that such should be stoned: but what sayest thou?* In other words, they were demanding an immediate answer while probably eyeing some stones in the vicinity preparatory to stoning her.

On the other hand, Jesus *milked* the process in order to drive home his message. Not only did they see their sins etched in the dirt by Jesus, It was said: "…he lifted up himself, and said unto them, he that is without sin let him cast the first stone at her,"(John 8:7). Ouch! Then he left them *hanging out to dry*.

Once again, he stooped down and wrote on the ground. By this time his message was taking deep root inside their minds as their names were once again etched in the dirt and associated with their sins. Yes, casting the first stone became problematic for the woman's accusers.

"And they which heard it, being convicted by their own conscience, went out one by one, beginning at the eldest, even to the last: and Jesus was left alone, and the woman in the midst.

When Jesus had lifted up himself and saw none but the woman he said unto her, Woman where are thine accusers? Hath no man condemned thee?" (John 8:9-10).

The woman at this point, no doubt was recovering from her guilt mixed with trepidation. She responded: "… No man, Lord.

And Jesus said unto her, Neither do I condemn thee: go, and sin no more," (John 8:11).

Jesus did not only send the woman away but cautioned her to *go and sin no more*.

Her accusers, on the other hand, pricked by their conscience, rejected mentally the cleansing power of Jesus. They opted to remain spiritually dead and fled.

On the other hand, the woman, the accused, and who they referred to as *such* was enjoying the newness of life. She found praises in her heart and on her lips.

TOTAL PRAISE

Meanwhile, her accusers were embarrassed, fled and worse of all held onto their sinful ways.

CHAPTER 20

ALL BELIEVERS ARE COMMANDED to praise God from whom all blessings flow. Praise to God is our acknowledgment of Him as the Supreme Being. Without Him we are nothing. In Genesis it is recorded: He made Man out of the dust of the ground. Breathed into him the breath of life and man became a living soul.

TOTAL PRAISE

You might be inclined to think that praise is just saying "thank you" but it goes beyond that attitude for what God has done. It is more like praising Him for who He is.

Praise originates from the heart and not merely from the lips. If your praise is all lip service it is bound to fall flat.

Our praise is manifested through our daily actions. That's why we can praise God anytime and anywhere. When we have a genuine relationship with Him our praise can be offered any place and at any time.

1 Peter 2:9 says, "But you are a chosen people, a royal priesthood, a holy nation, a people belonging to God, that you may declare the praises of him who called you out of darkness into his wonderful light."

Is his praise reflected when others look at you? Do they sense your attitude of praise?

Psalm 113:3 declares, "From the rising of the sun to the place where it sets, the name of the LORD is to be praised."

When we praise God we demonstrate our matchless faith in Him. Without Him, we can do nothing. Our deepest gratitude, honor, and glory belongs to Him.

According to one writer: *It is easy to praise God when the sun is shining, our children are making good grades in school, and we have received a promotion at work. But when the storm clouds gather, the grades start to slip, and the pink slips are read, the last thing we feel like doing is praising*

TOTAL PRAISE

God. Yet, this is the very time when we need to lift our voices to Him in praise.

CHAPTER 21

WHEN WE PRAISE GOD we ought to praise Him for His holiness, mercy, justice, grace, goodness, kindness, salvation and most of all His love towards us. Our praise to God should come as a result of a heart which is overflowing with joy. This joy may even come in lonely moments. At times when it seems like the whole world is against us. At times when we are cheated on, lied on, humiliated, cast aside, Unforgiven, chastised and rebuffed.

As our praise goes up to Him. He is moved. Stretches out that hand and says: "I've got you!" There is no other comforting feeling than knowing your best friend is there with you and for you when you are down and out. At times when you need a supernatural intervention.

There are times in our lives when we have done all that we can do. We have exhausted all of our options. We turned to prayer and our situation still looks futile. Even so, God knows best and praising Him for who He is proving we are content whatever our lot may be.

When peace, like a river, attendeth my way,
When sorrows like sea billows roll;
Whatever my lot, thou hast taught me to say,
It is well, it is well with my soul.

It is well with my soul;
It is well, it is well with my soul.

Though Satan should buffet, though trials should come,
Let this blest assurance control,
That Christ has regarded my helpless estate,
And has shed his own blood for my soul.

TOTAL PRAISE

My sin—O the bliss of this glorious thought!—
My sin, not in part, but the whole,
Is nailed to the cross and I bear it no more;
Praise the Lord, praise the Lord, O my soul!

O Lord, haste the day when the faith shall be sight,
The clouds be rolled back as a scroll,
The trump shall resound and the Lord shall descend;
"Even so"—it is well with my soul.

CHAPTER 22

IT WAS A LONG JOURNEY. The multitudes still pressed Him. The stalked. They begged. They badgered...Save me! Oh, save me!

One woman ambled through, sick with an issue of blood. Wellness had been her white-heated obsession for 12 years, to no avail. She reached out, touched the fringe of His garment. And Walla! She was healed.

TOTAL PRAISE

Those multitudes. Yes! Those multitudes. They left their homes at daybreak. Waiting to see Him, they brought no food. They brought no food and soon that negligent attitude wore on their stomachs. Pressuring their digestive tracks and soon lodged in their brains. How the heat of the desert scorched them. Their mouths were parched. Yet, they chanted, they cheered, and they chatted. Soon their saliva accumulated like glue onto their lips. While salty oxygen filled their lungs.

Andrew, one of His underlings yelled: "Here is a boy with five small barley loaves and two small fish." The Master commanded they sit on the grass.

"He took the loaves, gave thanks, and distributed to them." The allotment fed over 5,000 men with leftovers.

Later, someone screamed:

"Master, Lazarus is sick and near death. The Master seemed to be in no rush. I quizzed myself: *Is He going to let him die? Were there enough stripes on His lapel? Feathers in His cap or great deeds in His catalog?*

That messenger took off on foot. I breathlessly raced to the scene. Now with my sandal's straps flopping from side to side. My feet calloused. Beads of perspiration saturating my outer and undergarments.

I arrived. The Master stood tall staring at the gravestone. Tears soaked the handkerchiefs Mary and Martha used while they covering their nostrils.

TOTAL PRAISE

Inside my head, a voice echoed: *And now for the Late Breaking News. Let's take you directly to the scene at Lazarus' grave.*

The news came that Jesus
Please come fast
Lazarus is sick
And without your help he will not last
Mary and Martha watched their brother die
They waited for Jesus
He did not come
And they wondered why
The dead watch was over
Berried four days
Somebody said
"He'll soon be here, the Lord's on his way"
Martha ran to him and then she cried
"Lord if you had been here
You could have healed him
He'd still been alive"
But Lord, four days late
And all help is gone
Lord we don't understand
Why you waited so long
But his way is God's way
Not yours or mine
And isn't it great
When he's four days late
He's still on time
Jesus said

TOTAL PRAISE

"Martha, show me the grave"
But she said
"Lord, you don't understand
He's been there four days"
The gravestone was rolled back
Then Jesus cried
Lazarus come forward
Then somebody said
"He's alright, he's alive"
You may be fighting a battle of fear
You cry to the Lord
"I need you"
But he has not appeared
Friend don't be discouraged
'Cause he's still the same
He'll soon be here
He'll roll back the stone
And he'll call out your name
But he's four days late
And all help is gone
Lord we don't understand
Why you waited so long
But his way is God's way
Not yours or mine
And isn't it great
When he's four days late
He's still on time
He's still on time
Oh my God ...
When he's four days late

TOTAL PRAISE

He's still on time
He's still on time

About The Author

John A. Andrews hails from the beautiful Islands of St. Vincent and the Grenadines and resides in Hollywood, California. He is best known for his gritty and twisted writing style in his National Bestselling novel - Rude Buay ... The Unstoppable. He is in (2012) releasing this chronicle in the French edition and poised to release its sequel Rude Buay ... The Untouchable in March 2012.

Andrews moved from New York to Hollywood in 1996, to pursue his acting career. With early success, he excelled as a commercial actor. Then tragedy struck - a divorce, with Andrews, granted joint custody of his three sons, Jonathan, Jefferri, and Jamison, all under the age of five. That dream of becoming all he could be in the entertainment industry now took on nightmarish qualities.

In 2002, after avoiding bankruptcy and a twisted relationship at his modeling agency, he fell in love with a 1970s classic film, which he wanted to remake. Subsequent to locating the studio which held those rights, his request was denied. As a result, Andrews decided that he was going to write his own. Not knowing how to write and failing constantly at it, he inevitably recorded his first bestseller, Rude Buay ... The Unstoppable in 2010: a drug prevention chronicle, sending a strong message to teens and adults alike

Andrews is also a visionary, and a prolific author who has etched over two dozen titles including: Dare to Make a Difference - Success 101 for Teens, The 5 Steps To Changing Your Life, Spread Some Love - Relationships 101, Quotes Unlimited, How I Wrote 8 Books in One Year, The FIVE "Ps" for Teens, Total

TOTAL PRAISE

Commitment - The Mindset of Champions, and Whose Woman Was She? - A True Hollywood Story.

In 2007, Mr. Andrews a struggling actor and author etched his first book The 5 Steps to Changing Your Life. That title having much to do with changing one's thoughts, words, actions, character and changing the world. A book which he claims shaped his life as an author with now over two dozen published titles.

Andrews followed up his debut title with Spread Some Love - Relationships 101 in 2008, a title which he later turned into a one-hour docu-drama.

Additionally, during that year, Andrews wrote eight titles, including Total Commitment - The Mindset of Champions, Dare to Make A Difference - Success 101 for Teens, Spread Some Love - Relationships 101 (Workbook) and Quotes Unlimited.

After those publications in 2009, Andrews recorded his hit novel as well as Whose Woman Was She? and When the Dust Settles - I am Still Standing: his True Hollywood Story, now also being turned into a film.

New titles in the Personal Development genre include Quotes Unlimited Vol. II, The FIVE "Ps" For Teens, Dare to Make A Difference - Success 101 and Dare to Make A Difference - Success 101 - The Teacher's Guide.

His new translated titles include Chico Rudo ... El Imparable, Cuya Mujer Fue Ella? and Rude Buay ... The Unstoppable in Chinese.

Back in 2009, while writing the introduction of his debut book for teens: Dare To Make A Difference - Success 101 for Teens, Andrews visited the local bookstore. He discovered only 5 books in the Personal Development genre for teens while noticing hundreds of the same genre in the adult section. Sensing there was a lack of personal growth resources, focusing on youth 13-21, he published his teen book and soon thereafter founded Teen Success.

This organization is empowerment-based, designed to empower Teens in maximizing their full potential to be successful and contributing citizens in the world.

Andrews referred to as the man with "the golden voice" is a sought-after speaker on "Success" targeting young adults. He recently addressed teens in New York, Los Angeles, Hawaii and was the guest speaker at the 2011 Dr. Martin Luther King Jr. birthday celebrations in Eugene, Oregon.

John Andrews came from a home of educators; all five of his sisters taught school - two acquiring the status of school principals. Though self-educated, he understands the benefits of a great education and being all he can be. Two of his teenage sons are also writers. John spends most of his time writing, publishing books and traveling the country going on book tours.

Additionally, John Andrews is a screenwriter and producer and is in (2012) turning his bestselling novel into a film.

See more in:
HOW I RAISED MYSELF FROM FAILURE TO
SUCCESS IN HOLLYWOOD.

Visit: www.JohnAAndrews.com

Check out Upcoming Titles & New Releases...

ME TOO!
INSIDE THE CHURCH?

THE CONSPIRACY

FROM THE CREATOR OF:
THE CHURCH...A HOSPITAL?
THE CHURCH ON FIRE
&
TOTAL PRAISE

JOHN A. ANDREWS

PRESENTS

PREVIEWS OFF-BROADWAY - SPRING 2019

WRITTEN & DIRECTED
BY
JOHN A. ANDREWS

THE CHURCH ... A HOSPITAL?

JOHN A. ANDREWS

THE MUSICAL©

FROM THE CREATOR OF
RUDE BUAY
THE WHODUNIT CHRONICLES
&
THE CHURCH ON FIRE

SO MANY ARE TRYING TO GO TO HEAVEN
WITHOUT FIRST BUILDING A HEAVEN
HERE ON EARTH...
#1 INTERNATIONAL BESTSELLER

THE CHURCH ON FIRE

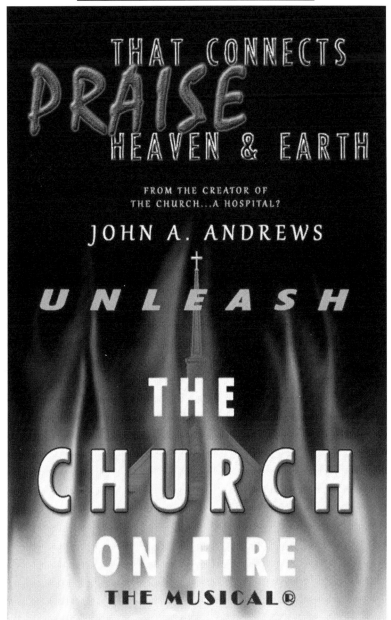

HOW I RAISED MYSELF FROM FAILURE TO SUCCESS IN HOLLYWOOD

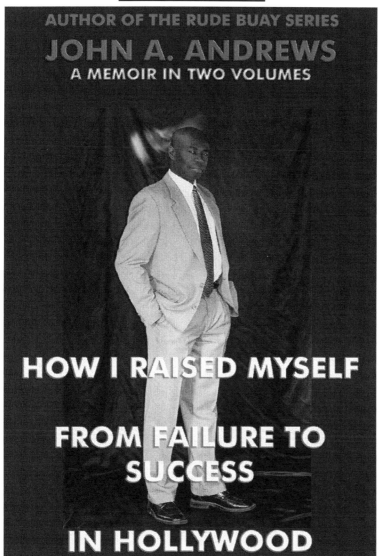

HOW I WROTE 8 BOOKS IN ONE YEAR

QUOTES UNLIMITED II

DARE TO MAKE A DIFFERENCE – SUCCESS 101

National Bestselling Author

Dare To Make
A
Difference

SUCCESS 101

JOHN A. ANDREWS

QUOTES UNLIMITED

THE 5 STEPS TO CHANGING YOUR LIFE

WHEN THE DUST SETTLES
I'M STILL STANDING

DARE TO MAKE A DIFFERENCE - SUCCESS 101 FOR TEENS

THE 5 Ps FOR TEENS

<u>SPREAD SOME LOVE – RELATIONSHIPS 101</u>

TOTAL PRAISE

<u>TOTAL COMMITMENT</u>

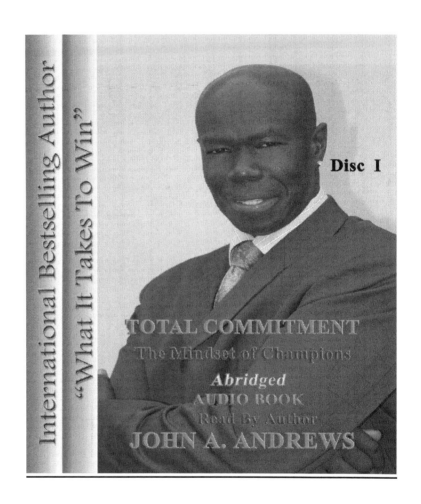

International Bestselling Author
"What It Takes To Win"

Disc II

TOTAL COMMITMENT
The Mindset of Champions
Abridged
AUDIO BOOK
Read By Author
JOHN A. ANDREWS

TOTAL PRAISE

VISIT: WWW.JOHNAANDREWS.COM

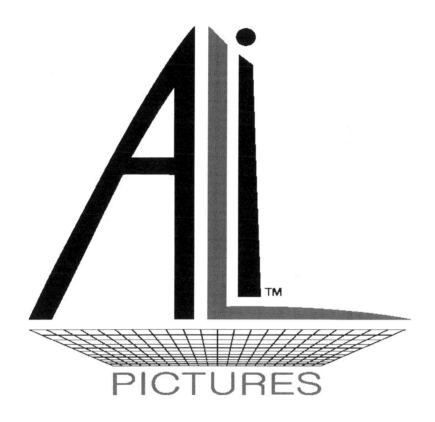

Optioned for A Musical Stage Play by:
A L I Pictures, LLC.

Unless otherwise indicated in the text, all Bible references used are from various versions of the Bible.

LIKE Us on FaceBook

https://www.facebook.com/JohnAAndrewsWritings/

TOTAL PRAISE

NOTES

NOTES

TOTAL PRAISE

NOTES

NOTES

TOTAL PRAISE

NOTES

TOTAL PRAISE

<u>NOTES</u>

NOTES

NOTES

48831006R00074

Made in the USA
Columbia, SC
16 January 2019